Personal Financial Planner
for use with

Personal Finance

Fourth Edition

Jack R. Kapoor
College of DuPage
Les R. Dlabay
Lake Forest College
Robert J. Hughes
Dallas County Community College

Developed by
Les R. Dlabay
Lake Forest College

IRWIN

Chicago • Bogotá • Boston • Buenos Aires • Caracas
London • Madrid • Mexico City • Sydney • Toronto

©Richard D. Irwin, a Times Mirror Higher Education Group, Inc. company,
1991, 1994 and 1996

Printed in the United States of America.

ISBN 0–256–14534–2

1 2 3 4 5 6 7 8 9 0 P 2 1 0 9 8 7 6 5

Personal Financial Planner

Preface

This *Personal Financial Planner* is packaged free with each copy of *Personal Finance*, Fourth Edition, by Kapoor, Dlabay, and Hughes purchased from Richard D. Irwin, Inc. This resource booklet is designed to help you create and implement a personal financial plan. The worksheets in this *Personal Financial Planner* are divided into the following main sections:

A — Personal Data and Goals
B — Career Planning
C — Money Management and Budgeting
D — Tax Planning
E — Banking Services
F — Consumer Credit
G — Consumer Buying
H — Housing
I — Insurance
J — Investments
K — Retirement and Estate Planning
L — Financial Plan Summary

Items to consider when using this Personal Financial Planner

1. Since this publication is designed to adapt to every personal financial situation, some of the sheets may be appropriate for you at this time, and not at other times in your life.

2. Each of the sheets in the first 10 sections is referenced to specific page numbers of *Personal Finance*, Fourth Edition, to help you better understand a topic. In addition, each sheet has one of the following symbols to highlight if it should be used in the planning, research, or summary phase of your financial decision making:

Planning Sheet

 Research Sheet

 Summary Sheet

3. Some sheets may need to be used more than once (such as preparing a personal cash flow statement or a budget). You are encouraged to photocopy additional sheets as needed.

4. Finally, remember personal financial planning is an ongoing activity. With the use of this booklet, the textbook, and your efforts, an organized and satisfying personal economic existence can be yours.

Note: Many of the calculation sheets in this booklet are available on the DOS version of *Personal Financial Planning Software.* A computerized version of this booklet is available for Windows® users.

Personal Financial Planner
Table of Contents

iv

Section A
Personal data and goals

The worksheets in this section are to be used with Chapter 1 of *Personal Finance*, Fourth Edition.

Sheet 1   Personal information sheet
Sheet 2   Financial institutions and advisors
Sheet 3   Goal setting sheet
Sheet 4   Time value of money calculations

2

Sheet 1 — Personal information sheet

Purpose: To provide quick reference for vital household data.
Instructions: Provide the personal and financial data requested below.

For use with
Personal Finance
Fourth Ed., Kapoor,
Dlabay & Hughes
Pages 5-6, 13-14

Name _____ _____

Birthdate _____ _____

Marital Status _____ _____

Address _____ _____

Phone _____ _____

Social Security No. _____ _____

Driver's License No. _____ _____

Place of Employment _____ _____

Address _____ _____

Phone _____ _____

Position _____ _____

Length of Service _____ _____

Checking Acct. No. _____ _____

Financial Inst. _____ _____

Address _____ _____

Phone _____ _____

Dependent data

Name	Birthdate	Relationship	Social Security No.

Sheet 2 — Financial institutions and advisors

Purpose: To create a directory of commonly used financial institutions and financial planning professionals.

Instructions: Provide the information in the spaces provided.

For use with *Personal Finance* Fourth Ed., Kapoor, Dlabay & Hughes Pages 8-9

Attorney

Name _____
Address _____
_____
Phone _____
Fax _____

Primary financial institution

Name _____
Address _____
_____
Phone _____
Fax _____
Checking
Acct. No. _____
Savings
Acct. No. _____
Loan No. _____

Insurance (home/auto)

Agent _____
Company _____
Address _____
_____
Phone _____
Fax _____
Policy No. _____

Credit card

Issuer _____
Address _____
_____
Phone _____
Fax _____
Acct. No. _____
Exp Date _____
Limit _____

Credit card

Issuer _____
Address _____
_____
Phone _____
Fax _____
Acct. No. _____
Exp Date _____
Limit _____

Tax preparer

Name _____
Firm _____
Address _____
_____
Phone _____
Fax _____

Insurance (life/health)

Agent _____

Company _____

Address _____

_____

Phone _____

Fax _____

Policy No. _____

Real estate agent

Name _____

Company _____

Address _____

_____

Phone _____

Fax _____

Investment broker

Name _____

Address _____

_____

Phone _____

Fax _____

Acct. No. _____

Investment company

Name _____

Address _____

_____

Phone _____

Fax _____

Acct. No. _____

Sheet 3 — Goal setting

Purpose: To identify personal financial goals and create an action plan.

Instructions: Based on personal and household needs and values, identify specific goals that require action.

For use with
Personal Finance
Fourth Ed., Kapoor,
Dlabay & Hughes
Pages 10-12

Short-term monetary goals (less than two years)

Description	Amount needed	Months to achieve	Action to be taken	Priority
Example: pay off credit card debt	$850	12	use money from pay raise	High

Intermediate and long-term monetary goals

Description	Amount needed	Months to achieve	Action to be taken	Priority

Non-monetary goals

Description	Time frame	Actions to be taken
Example: set up file for personal financial records and documents	next 2-3 months	locate all personal and financial records and documents; set up files for various spending, saving, borrowing categories

6

Sheet 4 — Time value of money calculations

Purpose: To calculate future and present value amounts related to financial planning decisions.

Instructions: Use a calculator or future or present value tables to compute the time value of money

For use with
Personal Finance
Fourth Ed., Kapoor, Dlabay & Hughes
Pages 18-21;78-79

Future value of a single amount
• to determine future value of a single amount
• to determine interest lost when cash purchase is made
(Use Exhibit C-1 in Reference C)

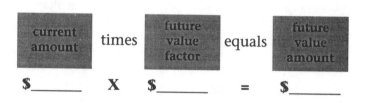

| current amount | times | future value factor | equals | future value amount |

$_____ X $_____ = $_____

Future value of a series of deposits
• to determine future values of regular savings deposits
• to determine future value of regular retirement deposits
(Use Exhibit C-2 in Reference C)

| regular deposit amount | times | future value of annuity factor | equals | future value amount |

$_____ X $_____ = $_____

Present value of a single amount
• to determine an amount to be deposited now that will grow to desired amount
(Use Exhibit C-3 in Reference C)

| future amount desired | times | present value factor | equals | present value amount |

$_____ X $_____ = $_____

Present value of a series of deposits
• to determine an amount that can be withdrawn on a regular basis
(Use Exhibit C-4 in Reference C)

| regular amount to be withdrawn | times | present value of annuity factor | equals | present value amount |

$_____ X $_____ = $_____

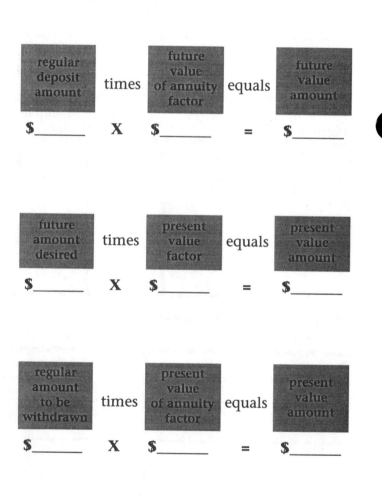

Section B
Career planning

The worksheets in this section are to be used with Chapter 2 of *Personal Finance*, Fourth Edition.

8

Sheet 5 — Career area research sheet

Purpose: To become familiar with work activities and career requirements for a field of employment.

Instructions: Using the *Career Occupational Outlook Handbook* and other information sources (library materials, interviews), obtain information related to one or more career areas of interest to you.

For use with
Personal Finance
Fourth Ed., Kapoor,
Dlabay & Hughes
Pages 31-36

Career area/job title		
Nature of the work general activities and duties		
Working conditions physical surroundings, hours, mental and physical demands		
Training and other qualifications		
Job outlook future prospect for employment in this field		
Earnings starting and advanced		
Additional information		
Other questions that require further research		
Sources of additional information publications, trade associations, professional organizations, government agencies		

Sheet 6 — Making career contacts

Purpose: To create a guide of professional contacts.

Instructions: Record the requested information for use in researching career areas and employment opportunities.

For use with
Personal Finance
Fourth Ed., Kapoor,
Dlabay & Hughes
Pages 37-38

Name _____

Organization _____

Address _____

_____

Phone _____

Fax _____ E-mail _____

Date of contact _____

Situation _____

Career situation

of contact _____

Areas of

specialization _____

Major

accomplishments _____

Name _____

Organization _____

Address _____

_____

Phone _____

Fax _____ E-mail _____

Date of contact _____

Situation _____

Career situation

of contact _____

Areas of

specialization _____

Major

accomplishments _____

10

Sheet 7 — Résumé worksheet

Purpose: To inventory your education, training, work background, and other experiences for use when preparing a résumé.

Instructions: List dates, organizations, and other data for each of the categories given below.

For use with
Personal Finance
Fourth Ed., Kapoor,
Dlabay & Hughes
Pages 40-42

Education

Degree/programs completed   School/location   Dates

Work experience

Title   Organization   Dates   Responsibilities

Other experience

Title   Organization   Dates   Responsibilities

Campus/community activities

Organization/location   Dates   Involvement

Honors/awards

Title   Organization/location   Dates

References

Name   Title   Organization   Address   Phone

Sheet 8 — Planning a cover letter

Purpose: To outline an employment cover letter.

Instructions: Prepare the preliminary draft of a cover letter for a specific employment position.

For use with *Personal Finance* Fourth Ed., Kapoor, Dlabay & Hughes Page 43

Name _____

Title _____

Organization _____

Address _____

_____

Phone _____

Fax _____ E-mail _____

Information about employment position available _____

Organizational information _____

INTRODUCTION: get attention of reader with distinctive skills or experience; or make reference to a mutual contact

DEVELOPMENT: emphasize how your experience, knowledge and skills will benefit the needs of the organization

CONCLUSION: request an interview; restate any distinctive qualities; tell how you may be contacted

12

Sheet 9 — Researching a prospective employer

Purpose: To obtain information about an organization for which an employment position is available.

Instructions: Use library research, informational interviews, and other sources to obtain the information requested below.

For use with
Personal Finance
Fourth Ed., Kapoor,
Dlabay & Hughes
Pages 43-44

Organization _____

Address _____

_____

Contact _____

Title _____

Phone _____

Fax _____ E-mail _____

Title of position _____

Major products, services and customers

Locations of main offices, factories and other facilities

Major historical developments of the company

Recent company and industry developments

Required skills and experience

Major responsibilities and duties

Employee benefits

Other comments

Sheet 10 — Preparing for an interview

Purpose: To organize information and ideas for a job interview.
Instructions: Prepare information for the items listed.

For use with
Personal Finance
Fourth Ed., Kapoor,
Dlabay & Hughes
Pages 43-45

Organization _____

Address _____

_____

Contact _____

Title _____

Phone _____

Fax _____ E-mail _____

Title of position _____

Date/time/location _____
of interview

Required skills and experience

Major responsibilities and duties

Questions you expect to be asked

Major ideas you plan to emphasize

Questions you plan to ask

Other comments

14

Sheet 11 — Employee benefits comparison

Purpose: To assess the financial and personal value of employment benefits.

Instructions: When comparing different employment situations, or when selecting benefits, consider the factors listed below.

For use with
Personal Finance
Fourth Ed., Kapoor,
Dlabay & Hughes
Pages 46-49

Organization		
Location		
Phone		
Contact/Title		
Health insurance Company/coverage Cost to be paid by employee		
Disability income insurance Company/coverage Cost to be paid by employee		
Life insurance Company/coverage Cost to be paid by employee		
Pension/retirement Employer contributions Vesting period Tax benefits Employee contributions		
Other benefits/ estimated market value • vacation time • tuition reimbursement • child/dependent care • other _____		

Sheet 12 — Career development & advancement

Purpose: To develop a plan for career advancement.

Instructions: Prepare responses for the items listed

For use with *Personal Finance* Fourth Ed., Kapoor, Dlabay & Hughes Pages 50-51

Current position _____

Address _____

_____

Phone _____

Fax _____ E-mail _____

Current responsibilities and duties

Accomplishments

Career goal within the next year

Required skills and experience

Plans to achieve that goal

Career goal within the next two years

Required skills and experience

Plans to achieve that goal

Career goal within the next five years

Required skills and experience

Plans to achieve that goal

Section C
Money management and budgeting

The worksheets in this section are to be used with Chapter 3 of *Personal Finance,* Fourth Edition.

18

Sheet 13 — Financial documents & records

Purpose: To develop a system for maintaining and storing personal financial documents and records.

Instructions: Indicate the location of the following financial records, and create files for the eight major categories of financial documents

For use with
Personal Finance
Fourth Ed., Kapoor,
Dlabay & Hughes
Pages 58-61

Item	Home file	Safe deposit box	Other (specify)
Money management records budget, financial statements			
Personal/employment records			
current résumé, social security card			
educational transcripts			
birth, marriage, divorce certificates			
citizenship, military papers			
adoption, custody papers			
Tax records			
Financial services/consumer credit records			
unused, cancelled checks			
savings, passbook statements			
savings certificates			
credit card information, statements			
credit contracts			
Consumer purchase, housing, and automobile records			
warranties, receipts			
owner's manuals			
lease or mortgage papers, title deed,			
property tax info			
automobile title			
auto registration			
auto service records			
Insurance records			
insurance policies			
home inventory			
medical information (health history)			
Investment records			
broker statements			
dividend reports			
stock/bond certificates			
rare coins, stamps and other collectibles			
Estate planning and retirement records			
will			
pension, social security info			

Sheet 14 — Personal balance sheet

Purpose: to determine your current financial position.

Instructions: List the current values of the asset categories below; list the amounts owed for various liabilities; subtract total liabilities from total assets to determine net worth.

For use with
Personal Finance
Fourth Ed., Kapoor,
Dlabay & Hughes
Pages 61-64

balance sheet as of _____

ASSETS

Liquid assets
Checking account balance _____
Savings/money market accounts, funds _____
Cash value of life insurance _____
Other _____ _____
Total liquid assets _____

Household assets and possessions
Current market value of home _____
Market value of automobiles _____
Furniture _____
Stereo, video, camera equipment _____
Jewelry _____
Other _____ _____
Other _____ _____
Total household assets _____

Investment assets
Savings certificates _____
Stocks and bonds _____
Individual retirement accounts _____
Mutual funds _____
Other _____ _____
Total investment assets _____

TOTAL ASSETS ▬▬▬▬▬

LIABILITIES

Current liabilities
Charge account and credit card balances _____
Loan balances _____
Other _____ _____
Other _____ _____
Total current liabilities _____

Long-term liabilities
Mortgage _____
Other _____ _____
Total long-term liabilities _____

TOTAL LIABILITIES ▬▬▬▬▬

NET WORTH ▬▬▬▬▬
(assets minus liabilities)

20

Sheet 15 — Personal cash flow statement

Purpose: To maintain a record of cash inflows and outflows for a month (or three months).

Instructions: Record inflows and outflows of cash for a one (or three) month period.

For use with
Personal Finance
Fourth Ed., Kapoor,
Dlabay & Hughes
Pages 64-68

for month ending _____

CASH INFLOWS

Salary (take-home) _____
Other income: _____
Other income: _____
TOTAL INCOME _____

CASH OUTFLOWS
Fixed expenses

Mortgage or rent _____
Loan payments _____
Insurance _____
Other _____ _____
Other _____ _____
Total fixed outflows _____

Variable expenses

Food _____
Clothing _____
Electricity _____
Telephone _____
Water _____
Transportation _____
Personal care _____
Medical expenses _____
Recreation/entertainment _____
Gifts _____
Donations _____
Other _____ _____
Other _____ _____
Total variable outflows _____

TOTAL OUTFLOWS _____

SURPLUS/DEFICIT _____

Allocation of surplus

Emergency fund savings _____
Financial goals savings _____
Other savings _____ _____

Sheet 16 — Cash budget

Purpose: To compare projected and actual spending for a one (or three) month period.

Instructions: Estimate projected spending based on your cash flow statement, and maintain records for actual spending for these same budget categories.

For use with
Personal Finance
Fourth Ed., Kapoor,
Dlabay & Hughes
Pages 71-73

	Budgeted amounts dollar	percent	Actual amounts	Variance
INCOME				
Salary				
Other _____				
Total income		100%		
EXPENSES				
Fixed expenses				
Mortgage or rent				
Property taxes				
Loan payments				
Insurance				
Other _____				
Total fixed expenses				
Emergency fund/ savings				
Emergency fund				
Savings for _____				
Savings for _____				
Total savings				
Variable expenses				
Food				
Utilities				
Clothing				
Transportation costs				
Personal care				
Medical and health care				
Entertainment				
Education				
Gifts/donations				
Miscellaneous				
Other _____				
Other _____				
Total variable expenses				
Total expenses		100%		

Sheet 17 — Annual budget summary

Purpose: To see an overview of spending patterns for a year.

Instructions: Record the monthly budget amount in the first column and actual monthly spending in the appropriate column.

For use with *Personal Finance* Fourth Ed., Kapoor, Dlabay & Hughes Pages 76-77

Expense	Budget	JAN	FEB	MAR	APR	MAY	JUN
Savings							
Mortgage/rent							
Housing costs							
Telephone							
Food (at home)							
Food (away)							
Clothing							
Transportation							
Credit payments							
Insurance							
Health care							
Recreation							
Reading/education							
Gifts/donations							
Miscellaneous							
Other _____							
Other _____							
TOTAL							

Year Totals

Expense	JUL	AUG	SEP	OCT	NOV	DEC	Actual	Budget
Savings								
Mortgage/rent								
Housing costs								
Telephone								
Food (at home)								
Food (away)								
Clothing								
Transportation								
Credit payments								
Insurance								
Health care								
Recreation								
Education								
Gifts/donations								
Miscellaneous								
Other _____								
Other _____								
TOTAL								

For use with
Personal Finance
Fourth Ed., Kapoor,
Dlabay & Hughes
Pages 78-79

Sheet 18 — College education cost analysis/savings plan

Purpose: To estimate future costs of college and calculate needed savings.

Instructions: Complete the information and calculations requested below.

Estimated cost of college education

Current cost of college education
(including tuition, fees, room, board,
books, travel and other expenses) $ _____

Future value for _____ years until starting $ _____
college at an expected annual inflation of
_____ percent (use future value of $1,
Exhibit B-1 in Appendix B)

Projected future cost of college adjusted for inflation $ _____

Estimated annual savings to

Projected future cost of college adjusted
for inflation   **A** $ _____

Future value of a series of deposits for
_____ years until starting college and
expected annual rate of return on saving
and investments of _____ percent (use
Exhibit B-2 in Appendix B)   **B** $ _____

Estimated annual deposit to achieve needed education fund

A divided by **B** $ _____

Section D
Tax planning

The worksheets in this section are to be used with Chapter 4 of *Personal Finance,* Fourth Edition.

Tax planning

26

Sheet 19 — Income tax estimate

Purpose: To estimate your current federal income tax liability.

Instructions: Based on last year's tax return, estimates for the current year, and current tax regulations and rates, estimate your current tax liability.

For use with
Personal Finance
Fourth Ed., Kapoor,
Dlabay & Hughes
Pages 87-95

Gross income (wages, salary, investment income, and other ordinary income) $ _____

LESS Adjustments to income (see current tax regulations)   - $ _____

EQUALS Adjusted gross income   = $ _____

LESS   Standard deduction   **OR**   Itemized deduction

medical expenses (exceeding 7.5% of AGI)	$ _____
state/local income, property taxes	$ _____
mortgage, home equity loan	$ _____
interest	$ _____
contributions	$ _____
casualty and theft losses	$ _____
moving expenses, job-related and miscellaneous expenses (exceeding 2% of AGI)	$ _____

AMOUNT - $ _____   **TOTAL**   - $ _____

LESS Personal exemptions   - $ _____

EQUALS Taxable income   = $ _____

Estimated tax (based on current tax tables or tax schedules) $ _____

LESS Tax credits   - $ _____

PLUS Other taxes   + $ _____

EQUALS Total tax liability   = $ _____

LESS Estimated withholding and payments   - $ _____

EQUALS Tax due (or refund)   = $ _____

Sheet 20 — Income tax preparer comparison

Purpose: To compare the services and costs of different income tax return preparation sources.

Instructions: Using advertisements and information from tax preparation services, obtain information for the following.

For use with *Personal Finance* Fourth Ed., Kapoor, Dlabay & Hughes Pages 103-104

	Local tax service	National tax service	Local accountant
Company name			
Address			
Telephone			
Cost of preparation of Form 1040EZ			
Cost of preparation of Form 1040A			
Cost of preparation of Form 1040 with Schedule A (itemized deductions)			
Cost of preparation of state or local tax return			
Assistance provided if IRS questions your return			
Other services provided			

28

Sheet 21 — Tax planning activities

Purpose: To consider actions that can prevent tax penalties and may result in tax savings.

Instructions: Consider which of the following actions are appropriate to your tax situation.

For use with
Personal Finance
Fourth Ed., Kapoor,
Dlabay & Hughes
Pages 87-102;107-110

	Action to be taken	N/A
Filing status/withholding		
Change filing status or exemptions due to changes in life situation		
Change amount of withholding due to changes in tax situation		
Plan to make estimated tax payments (due the 15th of April, June, September and January)		
Tax records/documents		
Organize home file for ease of maintaining and retrieving tax data		
Send current mailing address, correct social security number to IRS, place of employment, and other income sources		
Annual tax activities		
Be certain all needed data and current tax forms are available well before deadline		
Research uncertain tax areas		
Tax savings actions		
Consider tax-exempt and tax-deferred investments		
If you expect to have the same or lower tax rate next year, accelerate deductions into the current year		
If you expect to have the same or lower tax rate next year, delay the receipt of income until next year		
If you expect to have a higher tax rate next year, delay deductions since they will have a greater benefit		
If you expect to have a higher tax rate next year, accelerate the receipt of income to have it taxed at the current lower rate		
Start or increase use of tax-deferred retirement plans		
Other		

Section E
Banking services

The worksheets in this section are to be used with Chapter 5 of *Personal Finance,* Fourth Edition.

Sheet 22   Using savings to achieve financial goals
Sheet 23   Savings plan comparison
Sheet 24   Checking account comparison
Sheet 25   Checking account cost analysis
Sheet 26   Checking account reconciliation

Sheet 22 — Using savings to achieve financial goals

Purpose: To monitor savings for use in reaching financial goals.

Instructions: Record savings plan information along with the amount of your balance or income on a periodic basis.

For use with
Personal Finance
Fourth Ed., Kapoor,
Dlabay & Hughes
Pages 78-79;128-135

Regular savings account

Acct. No. _____

Financial institution

_____

Address _____

_____

Phone _____

Savings goal/Amount needed/Date needed:

Initial deposit:	**Date**	$
Balance:	**Date**	$
	Date	$
	Date	$
	Date	$

Certificates of deposit

Acct. No. _____

Financial institution

_____

Address _____

_____

Phone _____

Savings goal/Amount needed/Date needed:

Initial deposit:	**Date**	$
Balance:	**Date**	$
	Date	$
	Date	$
	Date	$

Money market fund/acct.

Acct. No. _____

Financial institution

_____

Address _____

_____

Phone _____

Savings goal/Amount needed/Date needed:

Initial deposit:	**Date**	$
Balance:	**Date**	$
	Date	$
	Date	$
	Date	$

U.S. Savings Bonds

Purchase location

_____

Address _____

_____

Phone _____

Savings goal/Amount needed/Date needed:

Purchase date:	Maturity:
Amount:	Maturity value:
Purchase date:	Maturity:
Amount:	Maturity value:

Other Savings

Acct. No. _____

Financial institution

_____

Address _____

_____

Phone _____

Savings goal/Amount needed/Date needed:

Initial deposit:	**Date**	$
Balance:	**Date**	$
	Date	$
	Date	$
	Date	$

Sheet 23 — Savings plan comparison

Purpose: To compare the benefits and costs associated with different savings plans.

Instructions: Analyze advertisements and contact various financial institutions to obtain the information requested below.

For use with
Personal Finance
Fourth Ed., Kapoor, Dlabay & Hughes
Pages 128-135

Type of savings plan (regular passbook account, special accounts, savings certificate, money market account, other)			
Financial institution			
Address			
Annual interest rate			
Annual percentage yield (APY)			
Frequency of compounding			
Interest computation method • day of deposit, day of withdrawal • average daily balance • low balance • other _____			
Insured by FDIC, NCUA, other			
Maximum amount insured			
Minimum initial deposit			
Minimum time period savings must be on deposit			
Penalties for early withdrawal			
Service charges/fees transaction fee for more than set number of withdrawals			
Other costs/fees			
"Free" gifts • item • amount of deposit • interest lost			

Sheet 24 — Checking account comparison

Purpose: To compare the benefits and costs associated with different checking accounts.

Instructions: Analyze advertisements and contact various financial institutions (banks, savings and loan associations, or credit unions) to obtain the information requested below.

For use with
Personal Finance
Fourth Ed., Kapoor, Dlabay & Hughes
Pages 136-138

Institution name			
Address			
Phone			
Type of account (regular checking, NOW account, share drafts, or other)			
Minimum balance for "free" checking			
Monthly service charge if minimum balance is not maintained			
Are "free" checking accounts available to full-time students?			
Other fees/costs printing of checks			
stop payment order			
overdrawn account			
certified check			
ATM, other charges			
Banking hours			
Location of branch offices and ATM terminals			

Sheet 25 — Checking account cost analysis

Purpose: To compare the inflows and outflows of a checking account

Instructions: Record the interest earned (inflows) and the costs and fees (outflows) as requested below. *Note: Not all items will apply to every checking account.*

For use with
Personal Finance
Fourth Ed., Kapoor,
Dlabay & Hughes
Pages 136-139

INFLOWS
Step 1

Multiply average monthly balance

by average rate of return
%
to determine annual earnings

OUTFLOWS
Step 2

Monthly service charge $
X 12 = $

Average number of checks written per month
X charge per check X 12 = $

Average number of deposits per month
X charge per deposit X 12 = $

Fee for dropping below minimum balance
X times below minimum = $

Lost interest:
opportunity cost %
X required minimum balance =
$

TOTAL ESTIMATED INFLOW
$

TOTAL ESTIMATED OUTFLOW
$

Estimated inflows less outflows=
= Net earnings for account
– Net cost for account

+/– $

Note: *This calculation does not take into account charges and fees for such services as overdrafts, stop payments, ATM use, and check printing. Be sure to also consider those costs when selecting a checking account.*

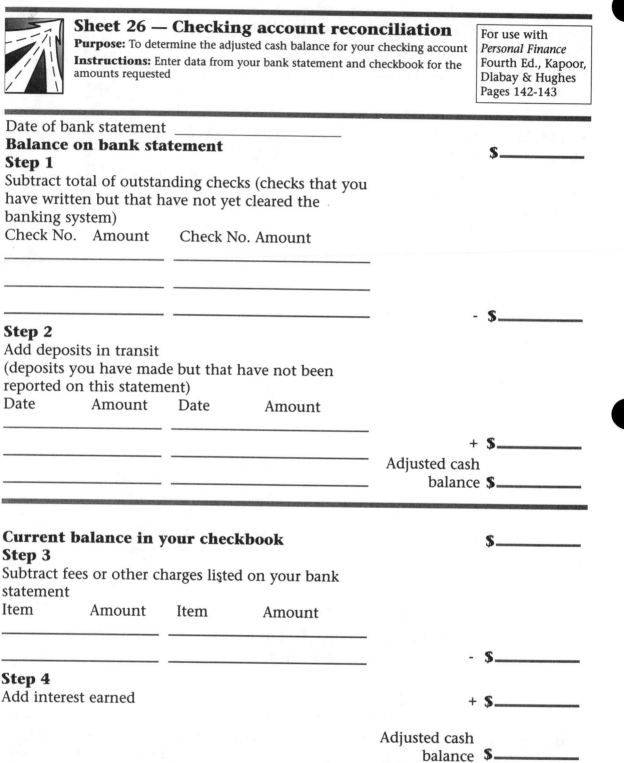

Sheet 26 — Checking account reconciliation

Purpose: To determine the adjusted cash balance for your checking account

Instructions: Enter data from your bank statement and checkbook for the amounts requested

For use with
Personal Finance
Fourth Ed., Kapoor,
Dlabay & Hughes
Pages 142-143

Date of bank statement _____

Balance on bank statement $_____

Step 1
Subtract total of outstanding checks (checks that you
have written but that have not yet cleared the
banking system)

Check No.   Amount   Check No. Amount

_____   _____

_____   _____

_____   _____   - $_____

Step 2
Add deposits in transit
(deposits you have made but that have not been
reported on this statement)

Date   Amount   Date   Amount

_____   _____

_____   _____   + $_____

_____   _____   Adjusted cash
                                                        balance $_____

Current balance in your checkbook $_____

Step 3
Subtract fees or other charges listed on your bank
statement

Item   Amount   Item   Amount

_____   _____

_____   _____   - $_____

Step 4
Add interest earned   + $_____

                                                        Adjusted cash
                                                        balance $_____

*The two adjusted balances should be the same; if not, carefully check your math and check
to see that deposits and checks recorded in your checkbook and on your statement are for the
correct amounts.*

Section F
Consumer credit

The worksheets in this section are to be used with Chapters 6 and 7 of *Personal Finance,* Fourth Edition.

Consumer credit

Sheet 27 — Consumer credit usage patterns

Purpose: To create a record of current consumer debt balances.

Instructions: Record account names, numbers, and payments for current consumer debts.

For use with
Personal Finance
Fourth Ed., Kapoor,
Dlabay & Hughes
Pages 158-159

Date _____

Automobile, education, personal and installment loans

Financial institution	Account number	Current balance	Monthly payment

Charge accounts and credit cards

Other loans (overdraft protection, home equity, life insurance loan)

Totals _____ _____

$$\text{Debt payment-to-income ratio} = \frac{\text{Total monthly payments}}{\text{net (after-tax) income}}$$

Sheet 28 — Credit card/charge account comparison

Purpose: To compare the benefits and costs associated with different credit cards and charge accounts.
Instructions: Analyze ads, credit applications, and contact various financial institutions to obtain the information requested below.

For use with
Personal Finance
Fourth Ed., Kapoor,
Dlabay & Hughes
Page 189

Type of credit/ charge account			
Name of company/ account			
Address			
Type of purchases which can be made			
Annual fee (if any)			
Annual percentage rate (APR) information Calculation method used			
Credit limit for new customers			
Minimum monthly payment			
Other costs: credit report late fee other _____			
Restrictions (age, minimum annual income)			
Other information for consumers to consider			

38

Sheet 29 — Consumer loan comparison

Purpose: To compare the costs associated with different sources of consumer loans.

Instructions: Contact or visit a bank, credit union, and consumer finance company to obtain information on a loan for a specific purpose.

For use with
Personal Finance
Fourth Ed., Kapoor, Dlabay & Hughes
Pages 152-55;184-88

Type of financial institution			
Name			
Address			
Phone			
Amount of down payment			
Length of loan (months)			
What collateral is required?			
Amount of monthly payment			
Total amount to be repaid (monthly amount x number of months + down payment)			
Total finance charge/cost of credit			
Annual percentage rate (APR)			
Other costs credit life insurance credit report other costs			
Is a co-signer required?			
Other information			

Section G
Consumer buying

The worksheets in this section are to be used with Chapters 8 and 10 of *Personal Finance,* Fourth Edition.

40

Sheet 30 — Comparing cash and credit for major purchases

Purpose: To compare the costs and benefits of cash and credit.

Instructions: When considering a major consumer purchase, complete the information requested below.

<table>
<tr><td>For use with
Personal Finance
Fourth Ed., Kapoor,
Dlabay & Hughes
Pages 184-88;222-24</td></tr>
</table>

Item/Description _____

Cash price

Selling price	$ _____
Sales tax	$ _____
Additional charges (delivery, setup, service contract)	$ _____
Discounts (employee, senior citizen or student discounts, discounts for paying cash)	$ _____
Net cost of item times percent interest that could be earned times years of use to determine opportunity cost	$ _____
Total financial & economic cost when paying cash	$ _____

Credit price

Down payment	$ _____
Financing: monthly payment times months	$ _____
Additional financing charges (application fee, credit report, credit life insurance)	$ _____
Product-related charges (delivery, setup)	$ _____
Discounts that may apply	$ _____
Total financial & economic cost when using credit	$ _____

Other considerations

Will cash used for the purchase be needed for other purposes?

Will this credit purchase result in financial difficulties?

Do alternatives exist for this purchasing and payment decision?

Note: Use Sheet 31 to compare brands, stores, features and prices when making a major consumer purchase.

Sheet 31 — Consumer purchase comparison

Purpose: To research and evaluate brands and store services for purchase of a major consumer item.

Instructions: When considering the purchase of a major consumer item, use ads, catalogs, store visits and other sources to obtain the information below.

For use with
Personal Finance
Fourth Ed., Kapoor,
Dlabay & Hughes
Pages 219-226

Product

Exact description (size, model, features, etc.)

Research the item in consumer periodicals with information regarding your product

**article/periodical
date/pages**

**article/periodical
date/pages**

What buying suggestions are presented in the articles?

Which brands are recommended in these articles? Why?

Contact or visit two or three stores that sell the product to obtain the following information:

	Store 1	Store 2	Store 3
Store name Address			
Phone			
Brand name/cost			
Product differences from item above			
Guarantee/warranty offered (describe)			

Which brand and at which store would you buy this product? Why?

42

Sheet 32 — Unit pricing worksheet

Purpose: To calculate the unit price for a consumer purchase.

Instructions: Use advertisements or information obtained during store visits to calculate and compare unit prices.

For use with
Personal Finance
Fourth Ed., Kapoor,
Dlabay & Hughes
Pages 228-229

Item (product or service) _____

Date	Store/Location	Brand	Total Price	÷ Size	=	Unit Price	Unit of Measurement

Highest unit price

Store

Date

Lowest unit price

Store

Date

Difference:

Wisest consumer buy/store

Reasons

Sheet 33 — Legal services cost comparison

Purpose: To compare costs of services from different sources of legal assistance.

Instructions: Contact various sources of legal services (lawyer, prepaid legal service, legal aid society) to compare costs and available services.

For use with *Personal Finance* Fourth Ed., Kapoor, Dlabay & Hughes Pages 234-236

Type of legal service			
Organization name Address			
Phone			
Contact person			
Recommended by			
Areas of specialization			
Cost of initial consultation			
simple will			
real estate closing			
Cost method for other services — flat fee, hourly rate, or contingency basis			
Other information			

Sheet 34 — Current and future transportation needs

Purpose: To assess current and future transportation.

Instructions: Based on current needs and expected needs, complete the information requested below.

For use with
Personal Finance
Fourth Ed., Kapoor,
Dlabay & Hughes
Pages 273-277

Current situation: Date _____

Vehicle 1

Year/Model _____

Mileage _____

Condition _____

Needed
repairs _____

Estimated annual costs

gas, oil, repairs _____

insurance _____

loan balance _____

Est. market value _____

Vehicle 2

Year/Model _____

Mileage _____

Condition _____

Needed
repairs _____

Estimated annual costs

gas, oil, repairs _____

insurance _____

loan balance _____

Est. market value _____

Expected and projected changes in transportation needs

Personal desires and concerns regarding current transportation

Analysis of future desired transportation situation
Description of new vehicle situation

Time when this situation is desired

Financing resources needed

Available and projected financial resources

Concerns that must be overcome

Realistic time when transportation of choice may be achieved

Sheet 35 — Used car purchase comparison

Purpose: To research and evaluate different types and sources of used cars.

Instructions: When considering a used car purchase, use advertisements and visits to new and used car dealers to obtain the information below.

For use with
Personal Finance
Fourth Ed., Kapoor,
Dlabay & Hughes
Pages 278-280

	Private party	Used car dealer	New car dealer
Automobile (year, make, model)			
Name			
Address			
Phone			
Cost			
Mileage			
Condition of auto			
Condition of tires			
Radio			
Air conditioning			
Other options			
Warranty (describe)			
Items in need of repair			
Inspection items: • any rust, major dents?			
• oil or fluid leaks?			
• condition of brakes?			
• proper operation of heater, wipers, other accessories?			
Other information			

46

<table>
<tr><td>

Sheet 36 — Buying vs. leasing an automobile

Purpose: To compare costs of buying and leasing an automobile or other vehicle.

Instructions: Obtain costs related to leasing and buying a vehicle.

</td><td>

For use with *Personal Finance* Fourth Ed., Kapoor, Dlabay & Hughes Pages 285-288

</td></tr>
</table>

Purchase costs

Total vehicle cost, including sales tax (**$** _____)

Down payment (or full amount if paying cash)   **$** _____

Monthly loan payment $ _____ times _____ month loan   **$** _____
(this item is zero if vehicle is not financed)

Opportunity cost of down payment (or total cost of the vehicle if bought for cash)
$_____ times number of years of financing/ownership
times _____ percent (interest rate which funds could earn)   **$** _____

Less: estimated value of vehicle at end of loan term/ownership **$** _____

TOTAL COST TO BUY   **$** _____

Leasing costs

Security deposit   **$** _____

Monthly lease payments $ _____ times _____ months   **$** _____

Opportunity cost of security deposit:

$ _____ times _____ years times _____ percent   **$** _____

End-of-lease charges (if applicable*)   **$** _____

TOTAL COST TO LEASE   **$** _____

With a closed-end lease, charges for extra mileage or excessive wear and tear; with an open-end lease, end-of-lease payment if appraised value is less than estimated ending value.

Sheet 37 — Auto ownership & operation costs

Purpose: To calculate or estimate the cost of owning and operating an automobile or other vehicle.

Instructions: Maintain records related to the cost categories listed below.

For use with
Personal Finance
Fourth Ed., Kapoor,
Dlabay & Hughes
Pages 288-290

Model year _____ Make, size, model _____

Fixed ownership costs

Depreciation*

Purchase price $ _____ divided by estimated life

of _____ years $ _____

Interest on auto loan

Annual cost of financing vehicle if buying on credit $ _____

Insurance for the vehicle

Annual cost of liability and property $ _____

License, registration fee and taxes

Cost of registering vehicle for state and city license fees $ _____

TOTAL FIXED COSTS $ _____

Variable costs

Gasoline

_____ estimated miles per year divided by _____

miles per gallon of _____ times

the average price of $_____ per gallon $ _____

Oil changes

Cost of regular oil changes during the year $ _____

Tires

Cost of tires purchased during the year $ _____

Maintenance/repairs

Cost of planned or other expected maintenance $ _____

Parking and tolls

Regular fees for parking and highway toll charges $ _____

TOTAL VARIABLE COSTS $ _____

Total costs $ _____

Divided by miles per year   _____

Equals cost per mile $ _____

* *This estimate of vehicle depreciation is based on a straight-line approach — equal depreciation each year; a more realistic approach would be larger amounts in the early years of ownership, such as 25-30% in the first year, 30-35% in the second year; most cars lose 90 percent of their value by the time they are seven years old.*

Section H
Housing

The worksheets in this section are to be used with Chapter 9 of *Personal Finance,* Fourth Edition.

Housing

Sheet 38 — Current and future housing needs

Purpose: To assess current and future plans for housing.

Instructions: Based on current and expected future needs, complete the information requested below.

For use with
Personal Finance
Fourth Ed., Kapoor,
Dlabay & Hughes
Pages 241-252

Current situation: **Date** _____

Renting

Location _____

Description _____

_____

Advantages _____

_____

Disadvantages _____

_____

Rent $ _____

Lease expiration _____

Buying

Location _____

Description _____

_____

Advantages _____

_____

Disadvantages _____

_____

Mortgage payment $ _____

Balance $ _____

Current market value _____

Expected and projected changes in housing needs

Personal desires and concerns regarding current housing situation

Analysis of future desired housing situation
Description of new housing situation

Time when this situation is desired

Financing resources needed/available

Concerns that must be overcome

Realistic time when transportation of choice may be achieved

Sheet 39 — Renting vs. buying housing

Purpose: To compare cost of renting and buying your place of residence

Instructions: Obtain estimates for comparable housing units for the data requested below.

For use with *Personal Finance* Fourth Ed., Kapoor, Dlabay & Hughes Pages 242-244

Rental costs

Annual rent payments (monthly rent $ _____ x 12) $ _____

Renter's insurance $ _____

Interest lost on security deposit $ _____

(deposit times after-tax savings acct. interest rate)

TOTAL ANNUAL COST OF RENTING $ _____

Buying costs

Annual mortgage payments $ _____

Property taxes (annual costs) $ _____

Homeowner's insurance (annual premium) $ _____

Estimated maintenance and repairs $ _____

After-tax interest lost because of down payment

and closing costs $ _____

LESS: *financial benefits of home ownership*

Growth in equity $- _____

Tax savings for mortgage interest

(annual mortgage interest times tax rate) $- _____

Tax savings for property taxes

(annual property taxes times tax rate) $- _____

Estimated annual depreciation $- _____

TOTAL ANNUAL COST OF BUYING $ _____

Sheet 40 — Apartment rental comparison

Purpose: To evaluate and compare rental housing alternatives.

Instructions: When in the market for an apartment, obtain information to compare costs and facilities of three apartments.

For use with
Personal Finance
Fourth Ed., Kapoor,
Dlabay & Hughes
Pages 245-248

Name of renting person or apartment building			
Address			
Phone			
Monthly rent			
Amount of security deposit			
Length of lease			
Utilities included in rent			
Parking facilities			
Storage area in building			
Laundry facilities			
Distance to schools			
Distance to public transportation			
Distance to shopping			
Pool, recreation area, other facilities			
Estimated other costs: Electric			
Telephone			
Gas			
Water			
Other costs			
Other information			

53

Sheet 41 — Housing affordability and mortgage qualification

Purpose: To estimate the amount of affordable mortgage payment, mortgage amount, and home purchase price.

Instructions: Enter the amounts requested, and perform the required calculations.

For use with *Personal Finance* Fourth Ed., Kapoor, Dlabay & Hughes Pages 255-257

Step 1
Determine your monthly gross income (annual income divided by 12) $ _____

Step 2
With a down payment of at least 10 percent, lenders use 28 percent of monthly gross income as a guideline for TIPI (taxes, insurance, principal and interest), 36 percent of monthly gross income as a guideline for TIPI plus other debt payments (enter .28 or .36)   x _____

Step 3
Subtract other debt payments (such as payments on an auto loan), if applicable   − _____
Subtract estimated monthly costs of property taxes and homeowners insurance   − _____
Affordable monthly mortgage payment $ _____

Step 4
Divide this amount by the monthly mortgage payment per $1,000 based on current mortgage rates (see Exhibit 9-9, text p. 257). For example, for a 10 percent, 30-year loan, the number would be $8.78)   ÷ _____
Multiply by $1,000.   x $ 1,000
Affordable mortgage amount $ _____

Step 5
Divide your affordable mortgage amount by 1 minus the fractional portion of your down payment (for example, 0.9 for a 10 percent down payment)   ÷ _____
Affordable home purchase price $ _____

Note: The two ratios used by lending institutions (Step 2) and other loan requirements are likely to vary based on a variety of factors, including the type of mortgage, the amount of the down payment, your income level, and current interest rates. If you have other debts, lenders will calculate both ratios and then use the one that allows you greater flexibility in borrowing.

54

Sheet 42 — Mortgage company comparison

Purpose: To compare the services and costs for different home mortgage sources.

Instructions: When obtaining a mortgage, obtain the information requested below from different mortgage companies.

For use with *Personal Finance* Fourth Ed., Kapoor, Dlabay & Hughes Pages 258-263

Amount of mortgage $ _____ Down payment $ _____ Years ____

Company		
Address		
Phone		
Contact person		
Application, credit report, property appraisal fees		
Loan origination fee		
Other fees, charges (commitment, title, tax transfer)		
Fixed rate mortgage		
Monthly payment		
Discount points		
Adjustable rate mortgage		
• time until first rate charge • frequency of rate charge		
Monthly payment		
Discount points		
Payment cap		
Interest rate cap		
Rate index used		
Commitment period		
Other information		

Sheet 43 — Mortgage refinance analysis

Purpose: To determine savings associated with refinancing a mortgage

Instructions: Record refinancing costs and amount saved with new mortgage in the areas provided.

For use with
Personal Finance
Fourth Ed., Kapoor,
Dlabay & Hughes
Page 263

Costs of refinancing:

Points	**$** _____	
Application fee	**$** _____	
Credit report	**$** _____	
Attorney fees	**$** _____	
Title search	**$** _____	
Title insurance	**$** _____	
Appraisal fee	**$** _____	
Inspection fee	**$** _____	
Other fees	**$** _____	
Total refinancing costs		**A** $ _____

Monthly savings:

Current monthly mortgage payment	**$** _____	
LESS: new monthly payment	**$** _____	
Monthly savings		**B** $ _____

Number of months to cover finance costs

Refinance costs (A) divided by monthly savings (B)

_____ months

Section I
Insurance

The worksheets in this section are to be used with Chapters 11-14 of *Personal Finance,* Fourth Edition.

58

Sheet 44 — Current insurance policies and needs

Purpose: To establish a record of current and needed insurance coverage.

Instructions: List current insurance policies and areas where new or additional coverage is needed.

For use with
Personal Finance
Fourth Ed., Kapoor,
Dlabay & Hughes
Pages 306-309

Current coverage	Needed coverage
Property insurance Company Policy No. Coverage amounts Deductible Annual premium Agent Address Phone	
Automobile insurance Company Policy No. Coverage amounts Deductible Annual premium Agent Address Phone	
Disability income insurance Company Policy No. Coverage Contact Phone	
Health insurance Company Policy No. Policy provisions Contact Phone	
Life insurance Company Policy No. Type of policy Amount of coverage Cash value Agent Phone	

Sheet 45 — Home inventory

Purpose: To create a record of personal belongings for use when settling home insurance claims.

Instructions: For areas of the home, list your possessions including a description (model, serial number), cost and date of acquisition.

For use with
Personal Finance
Fourth Ed., Kapoor,
Dlabay & Hughes
Pages 325-327

Item, description	Cost	Date acquired
Attic		
Bathroom		
Bedrooms		
Family room		
Living room		
Hallways		
Kitchen		
Dining room		
Basement		
Garage		
Other items		

Sheet 46 — Determining needed property insurance

Purpose: To determine property insurance needed for a home or apartment.

Instructions: Estimate the value and your needs for the categories below.

For use with
Personal Finance
Fourth Ed., Kapoor,
Dlabay & Hughes
Pages 330-332

Real property *(this section not applicable to renters)*

Current replacement value of home $ _____

Personal property

Estimated value of appliances, furniture, clothing and
other household items (conduct an inventory) $ _____

Type of coverage for personal property
    actual cash value ▪
    replacement value ▪

Additional coverage for items with limits on standard personal property coverage
such as jewelry, firearms, silverware, photographic, electronic and computer
equipment

Item	Amount

Personal liability

Amount of additional personal liability coverage
desired for possible personal injury claims $ _____

Specialized coverages

If appropriate, investigate flood or earthquake coverage
excluded from home insurance policies $ _____

*Note: Use Sheet 47 to compare companies, coverages and costs for apartment or home
insurance.*

Sheet 47 — Apartment/home insurance comparison

Purpose: To research and compare companies, coverages and costs for apartment or home insurance.
Instructions: Contact three insurance agents to obtain the information requested below.

For use with
Personal Finance
Fourth Ed., Kapoor,
Dlabay & Hughes
Pages 328-332

Type of building: ■ apartment ■ home ■ condominium
Location: _____
Type of construction _____ Age of building _____

Company name			
Agent's name, address and phone			
Coverage: Dwelling $ Other structures $ (does not apply to apartment/condo coverage)	**Premium**	**Premium**	**Premium**
Personal property $			
Additional living expenses $			
Personal liability Bodily injury $ Property damage $			
Medical payments per person $ per accident $			
Deductible amount			
Other coverage $			
Service charges or fees			
TOTAL PREMIUM			

Sheet 48 — Automobile insurance cost comparison

Purpose: To research and compare companies, coverages and costs for auto insurance.

Instructions: Contact three insurance agents to obtain the information requested below.

For use with
Personal Finance
Fourth Ed., Kapoor,
Dlabay & Hughes
Pages 333-341

Automobile (year, make, model, engine size):

Driver's age: Sex: Total miles driven in a year:

Full- or part-time driver?   Number of miles driven to work:

Driver's education completed?

Accidents or violations with the past three years?

Company name			
Agent's name, address and phone			
Policy length (6 months, 1 year)			
Coverage:	**Premium**	**Premium**	**Premium**
Bodily injury liability per person $ per accident $			
Property damage liab. per accident $			
Collision deductible $			
Comprehensive deductible $			
Medical payments per person $			
Uninsured motorist per person $ per accident $			
Other coverage			
Service charges			
TOTAL PREMIUM			

Sheet 49 — Disability income insurance needs

Purpose: To determine financial needs and insurance coverage related to employment disability situations.

Instructions: Use the categories below to determine your potential income needs and disability insurance coverage.

For use with
Personal Finance
Fourth Ed., Kapoor,
Dlabay & Hughes
Pages 352-357

Monthly expenses

	Current	When disabled
Mortgage (or rent)	$ _____	$ _____
Utilities	$ _____	$ _____
Food	$ _____	$ _____
Clothing	$ _____	$ _____
Insurance payments	$ _____	$ _____
Debt payments	$ _____	$ _____
Auto/transportation	$ _____	$ _____
Medical/dental care	$ _____	$ _____
Education	$ _____	$ _____
Personal allowances	$ _____	$ _____
Recreation/entertainment	$ _____	$ _____
Contributions, donations	$ _____	$ _____

TOTAL MONTHLY EXPENSES WHEN DISABLED $ _____

Substitute income

Monthly benefit*

Group disability insurance	$ _____
Social security	$ _____
State disability insurance	$ _____
Workers' compensation	$ _____
Credit disability insurance (in some auto loan or home mortgages	$ _____
Other income (investments, etc.)	$ _____

TOTAL PROJECTED INCOME WHEN DISABLED $ _____

If projected income when disabled is less than expenses, additional disability income insurance should be considered.

* Most disability insurance programs have a waiting period before benefits start, and may have a limit as to how long benefits are received.

64

Sheet 50 — Assessing current and needed health care insurance

Purpose: To assess current and needed medical and health care insurance.
Instructions: Investigate your existing medical and health insurance, and determine the need for additional coverages.

For use with
Personal Finance
Fourth Ed., Kapoor,
Dlabay & Hughes
Pages 357-363

Insurance company

Address

Type of insurance ■ individual health policy ■ group health policy

Premium amount (monthly/quarter/semi-annual/annual)

Main coverages

Amount of coverage for
hospital costs
surgery costs
physician's fees
lab tests
out-patient expenses
maternity
major medical

Other items covered/amounts

Policy restrictions (deductibles, co-insurance, maximum limits)

Items not covered by this insurance

Of items not covered, would supplemental coverage be appropriate for your personal situation?

What actions related to your current (or proposed additional) coverage are necessary?

Sheet 51 — Life insurance needs

Purpose: To estimate life insurance coverage needed to cover expected expenses and future family living costs.

Instructions: Estimate the amounts requested for the categories listed.

For use with
Personal Finance
Fourth Ed., Kapoor,
Dlabay & Hughes
Pages 381-383

Household expenses to be covered

Final expenses (funeral, estate taxes, etc.)   **1 $** _____
Payment of consumer debt amounts   **2 $** _____
Emergency fund   **3 $** _____
College fund   **4 $** _____
Expected living expenses:
    Average living expenses $ _____
    Spouse's income after taxes $- _____
    Annual Social Security benefits $- _____
    Net annual living expenses $ _____
    Years until spouse is 90 $ _____
    Investment rate factor (see below) $ _____
    Total living expenses
    (net annual expenses times
    investment rate factor)   **5 $** _____

Total monetary needs (1+2+3+4+5) $ _____
LESS: Total current investments $- _____
Life insurance needs $ _____

Investment rate factors

Years until spouse is 90	25	30	35	40	45	50	55	60
conservative investment	20	22	25	27	30	31	33	35
aggressive investment	16	17	19	20	21	21	22	23

Note: Use Sheet 52 to compare life insurance policies

Sheet 52 — Life insurance policy comparison

Purpose: To research and compare companies, coverages, and costs for different life insurance policies.

Instructions: Analyze ads and contact life insurance agents to obtain the information requested below.

For use with
Personal Finance
Fourth Ed., Kapoor,
Dlabay & Hughes
Pages 384-395

AGE:

Company			
Agent's name, address and phone			
Type of insurance (term, straight/whole, limited payment, endowment, universal)			
Type of policy (individual, group)			
Amount of coverage			
Frequency of payment (monthly, quarterly, semi-annual, annual)			
Premium amount			
Other costs: • service charges • physical exam			
Rate of return (annual percentage increase in cash value; not applicable for term policies)			
Benefits of insurance as stated in ad or by agent			
Potential problems or disadvantages of this coverage			

Section J
Investments

The worksheets in this section are to be used with Chapters 15-19 of *Personal Finance,* Fourth Edition.

Investments

Sheet 53 — Setting investment objectives

Purpose: To determine specific goals for an investment program.

Instructions: Based on short and long term objectives for your investment efforts, enter the items requested below.

For use with
Personal Finance
Fourth Ed., Kapoor,
Dlabay & Hughes
Pages 409-413

Description of financial need	Amount	Date needed	Investment goal (safety, growth, income)	Level of risk (high, medium, low)	Possible investments to achieve this goal

Note: Sheets 55, 56, and 57 may be used to implement specific investment plans to achieve these goals.

Sheet 54 — Assessing risk for investments

Purpose: To assess the risk of various investments in relation to your personal risk tolerance and financial goals.

Instructions: List various investments you are considering based on the type and level of risk associated with each.

For use with *Personal Finance* Fourth Ed., Kapoor, Dlabay & Hughes Pages 414-418

Level of risk	Loss of market value (market risk)	Type of risk		
		Inflation risk	Interest rate risk	Liquidity risk
High risk				
Moderate risk				
Low risk				

Sheet 55 — Using stocks to achieve financial goals

Purpose: To plan stock investments for specific financial goals.

Instructions: Use current and projected stock values and dividends to create an investment plan for achieving a goal..

For use with
Personal Finance
Fourth Ed., Kapoor,
Dlabay & Hughes
Pages 445-460

Financial goal/amount

STOCK
Date:
Company:
Purchase price per share: $
Number of shares:
Total cost including commission: $

Value 1	**Value 2**	**Value 3**
Date:	Date:	Date:
Price per share: $	Price per share: $	Price per share: $
Total value: $	Total value: $	Total value: $

Financial goal/amount

STOCK
Date:
Company:
Purchase price per share: $
Number of shares:
Total cost including commission: $

Value 1	**Value 2**	**Value 3**
Date:	Date:	Date:
Price per share: $	Price per share: $	Price per share: $
Total value: $	Total value: $	Total value: $

Financial goal/amount

STOCK
Date:
Company:
Purchase price per share: $
Number of shares:
Total cost including commission: $

Value 1	**Value 2**	**Value 3**
Date:	Date:	Date:
Price per share: $	Price per share: $	Price per share: $
Total value: $	Total value: $	Total value: $

NOTE: Different stocks can be used for each financial goal, or a portfolio of several stocks can be used for a single financial goal.

Sheet 56 — Using bonds to achieve financial goals

Purpose: To plan bond investments to achieve specific financial goals.

Instructions: Use current and projected interest income and bond prices to create an investment plan for achieving a goal.

For use with
Personal Finance
Fourth Ed., Kapoor,
Dlabay & Hughes
Pages 479-490

Financial goal/amount

CORPORATE BOND

Date: Organization: Purchase price: $
Number of bonds:
Interest rate annual amount _____%: $
Total cost including commission: $

Value 1	**Value 2**	**Value 3**
Date:	Date:	Date:
Price per bond: $	Price per bond: $	Price per bond: $
Total value: $	Total value: $	Total value: $
Interest earned: $	Interest earned: $	Interest earned: $

Financial goal/amount

CORPORATE BOND

Date: Organization: Purchase price: $
Number of bonds:
Interest rate annual amount _____%: $
Total cost including commission: $

Value 1	**Value 2**	**Value 3**
Date:	Date:	Date:
Price per bond: $	Price per bond: $	Price per bond: $
Total value: $	Total value: $	Total value: $
Interest earned: $	Interest earned: $	Interest earned: $

Financial goal/amount

CORPORATE BOND

Date: Organization: Purchase price: $
Number of bonds:
Interest rate annual amount _____%: $
Total cost including commission: $

Value 1	**Value 2**	**Value 3**
Date:	Date:	Date:
Price per bond: $	Price per bond: $	Price per bond: $
Total value: $	Total value: $	Total value: $
Interest earned: $	Interest earned: $	Interest earned: $

NOTE: Different investments can be used for each financial goal, or a portfolio of several investments can be used for a single financial goal.

Sheet 57 — Using mutual funds and other investments

Purpose: To plan for using mutual funds and other investments to achieve specific financial goals.

Instructions: Use current and projected investment values and incomes to create an investment plan for achieving a financial goal.

For use with
Personal Finance
Fourth Ed., Kapoor, Dlabay & Hughes
Pages 499-515;532-35

Financial goal/amount

MUTUAL FUND

Date: Company:
Type of fund: Purchase price: $
Number of shares:
Total cost including fees: $

Value 1	**Value 2**	**Value 3**
Date:	Date:	Date:
NAV (net asset value)	NAV (net asset value)	NAV (net asset value)
$	$	$
Total value: $	Total value: $	Total value: $

Financial goal/amount

MUTUAL FUND

Date: Company:
Type of fund: Purchase price: $
Number of shares:
Total cost including fees: $

Value 1	**Value 2**	**Value 3**
Date:	Date:	Date:
NAV (net asset value)	NAV (net asset value)	NAV (net asset value)
$	$	$
Total value: $	Total value: $	Total value: $

Financial goal/amount

OTHER INVESTMENT

Date:
Contact: Purchase price: $
Phone:
Total cost including fees: $

Value 1	**Value 2**	**Value 3**
Date:	Date:	Date:
Market value	Market value	Market value
$	$	$
Income: $	Income: $	Income: $

NOTE: Different investments can be used for each financial goal, or a portfolio of several investments can be used for a single financial goal.

Sheet 58 — Investment broker comparison

Purpose: To compare the benefits and costs of different investment brokers.

Instructions: Compare the services of an investment broker based on the factors listed below.

For use with *Personal Finance* Fourth Ed., Kapoor, Dlabay & Hughes Pages 455-456

Broker's name		
Organization		
Address		
Phone		
Years of experience		
Education and training		
Areas of specialization		
Certifications held		
Professional affiliations		
Employer's stock exchange and financial market affiliations		
Information services offered		
Minimum commission charge		
Commission on 100 shares of stock at $50/share		
Fees for other investments: • corporate bonds • mutual funds • stock options		
Other fees: • annual account fee • inactivity fee • other		

Section K
Retirement & estate planning

The worksheets in this section are to be used with Chapters 20-21 of *Personal Finance*, Fourth Edition.

Retirement planning

Sheet 59 — Retirement housing and lifestyle planning

Purpose: To consider housing alternatives for retirement living, and to plan retirement activities.
Instructions: Evaluate current and expected needs and interests based on the items below.

For use with
Personal Finance
Fourth Ed., Kapoor,
Dlabay & Hughes
Pages 552-554

Retirement housing plans

Description of current housing situation (size, facilities, location)

Time until retirement _____ years

Description of retirement housing needs

Checklist of retirement housing alternatives

_____ present home	_____ professional companionship arrangement
_____ housesharing	_____ commercial rental
_____ accessory apartment	_____ board and care home
_____ elder cottage housing	_____ congregate housing
_____ rooming house	_____ continuing care retirement community
_____ single-room occupancy	_____ nursing home
_____ caretaker arrangement	

Personal and financial factors that will influence the retirement housing decision

Financial planning actions to be taken related to retirement housing

Retirement activities

What plans do you have to work part-time or do volunteer work?

What recreational activities do you plan to continue or start?
(Location, training, equipment needs)

What plans do you have for travel or educational study?

Sheet 60 — Retirement plan comparison

Purpose: To compare benefits and costs for different retirement plans (401K, IRA, Keogh).

Instructions: Analyze advertisements and articles, and contact your employer and financial institutions to obtain the information below.

For use with
Personal Finance
Fourth Ed., Kapoor,
Dlabay & Hughes
Pages 555-563

Type of plan			
Name of financial institution or employer			
Address			
Type of investments (savings certificate, stocks, bonds)			
Minimum initial deposit			
Minimum addtl. deposits			
Employer contributions			
Current rate of return			
Service charges/fees			
Safety Insured? By whom? Amount			
Payroll deduction available			
Tax benefits			
Penalty for early withdrawal: • IRS penalty (10%) • other penalties			
Other features or restrictions			
SAMPLE ACCOUNT GROWTH Depositing $2,000 a year for _____ years will grow to $ _____			

78

Sheet 61 — Forecasting retirement income

Purpose: To determine the amount needed to save each year to have the necessary funds to cover retirement living costs.

Instructions: Estimate the information requested below.

> For use with
> *Personal Finance*
> Fourth Ed.
> Pages 549-552;
> 555-571

Estimated annual retirement living expenses

Estimated annual living expenses
if you retired today $_____

Future value for ____ years until
retirement at expected annual income
of ____ % (use future value of $1,
Exhibit C-1 of Reference C)   x _____

**Projected annual retirement living expenses
adjusted for inflation (A)** $ _____

Estimated annual income at retirement

Social security income $ _____

Company pension, personal retirement
account income $ _____

Investment and other income $ _____

Total retirement income (B) $ _____

Additional retirement plan contributions (if B is less than A)

Annual shortfall of income after
retirement (A-B) $ _____

Expected annual rate of return on
invested funds after retirement,
percentage expressed as a decimal $ _____

**Needed investment fund after retirement
A-B (C)** $ _____

Future value factor of a series of deposits for ___ years
until retirement and an expected annual rate of return
before retirement of ____ % (Use Exhibit C-2 in
Reference C) **(D)** $ _____

**Annual deposit to achieve needed investment fund
(C divided by D)** $ _____

Sheet 62 — Estate planning activities

Purpose: To develop a plan for estate planning and related financial activities.

Instructions: Respond to the following questions as a basis for making and implementing an estate plan.

For use with
Personal Finance
Fourth Ed., Kapoor,
Dlabay & Hughes
Pages 577-579

Are your financial records, including recent tax forms, insurance policies, and investment and housing documents, organized and easily accessible?	
Do you have a safe-deposit box? Where is it located? Where is the key?	
Location of life insurance policies. Name and address of insurance company and agent.	
Is your will current? Location of copies of your will. Name and address of your lawyer.	
Name and address of your executor.	
Do you have a listing of the current value of assets owned and liabilities outstanding?	
Have any funeral and burial arrangements been made?	
Have you created any trusts? Name and location of financial institution.	
Do you have any current information on gift and estate taxes?	
Have you prepared a letter of last instructions? Where is it located?	

Sheet 63 — Estate tax projection and settlement costs

Purpose: To estimate the estate tax based on your financial situation.

Instructions: Enter the data requested below to calculate the tax based on current tax rates.

For use with
Personal Finance
Fourth Ed., Kapoor,
Dlabay & Hughes
Pages 594-598

Gross estate values

Personal property	$ _____
Real estate	$ _____
Joint ownership	$ _____
Business interests	$ _____
Life insurance	$ _____
Employee benefits	$ _____
Controlled gifts/trusts	$ _____
Prior taxable gifts	$ _____
Total estate values	$ _____

Deductible debts, costs, expenses

Mortgages and secured loans	$ _____
Unsecured notes and loans	$ _____
Bills and accounts payable	$ _____
Funeral and medical expenses	$ _____
Probate administration costs	$ _____
Total deductions	-$ _____
Marital deduction	-$ _____
Taxable estate	= $ _____

GROSS ESTATE TAX* $ _____

Allowable credits

Unified credit	$ _____
Gift tax credit	$ _____
State tax credit	$ _____
Foreign tax credit	$ _____
Prior tax credit	$ _____
Total tax credits	-$ _____
NET ESTATE TAX	$ _____

*Consult the Internal Revenue Service for current rates and regulations related to estate taxes.

Section L
Financial plan summary

The following worksheets are designed to summarize the actions needed to assess, plan, and achieve your personal financial goals:

Sheet 64   Financial data summary
Sheet 65   Savings/investment portfolio summary
Sheet 66   Progress check on major financial goals and activities
Sheet 67   Summary for money management, budgeting
                  and tax planning
Sheet 68   Summary for banking services and consumer credit
Sheet 69   Summary for consumer buying and housing
Sheet 70   Summary for insurance
Sheet 71   Summary for investments
Sheet 72   Summary for retirement and estate planning

As you complete the various sheets in the previous sections, transfer financial data, goals, and planned actions to the summary sheets in this section. For example:

Sheet	Actions to be taken	Planned completion date	Completed (√)
13 (financial documents & records)	locate and organize all personal financial documents	within 2-3 months	
19 (current income tax estimate)	sort current tax data, compute estimate to determine tax amount	February 15	√

Sheet 64 — Financial data summary

DATE					
Balance sheet summary					
Assets					
Liabilities					
Net worth					
Cash flow summary					
Inflows					
Outflows					
Surplus/deficit					
Budget summary					
Budget					
Actual					
Variance					
DATE					
Balance sheet summary					
Assets					
Liabilities					
Net worth					
Cash flow summary					
Inflows					
Outflows					
Surplus/deficit					
Budget summary					
Budget					
Actual					
Variance					

Sheet 65 — Savings/investment portfolio summary

Description	Organization contact/phone	Purchase price/date	Value/ date	Value/ date	Value/ date	Value/ date

Sheet 66 — Progress check on major financial goals and activities

Some financial planning activities require short-term perspective. Other activities may require continued efforts over a long period of time, such as purchasing a vacation home. This sheet is designed to help you monitor these long-term, ongoing financial activities.

Major financial objective	Desired completion date	Initial actions and date	Progress checks (date, progress made, and other actions to be taken)

Sheet 67 — Summary for money management, budgeting and tax planning activities
(Text Chapters 3-4)

Sheet	Actions to be taken	Planned completion date	Completed (√)

86

Sheet 68 — Summary for banking services and consumer credit activities
(Text Chapters 5-7)

Sheet	Actions to be taken	Planned completion date	Completed (√)

Sheet 69 — Summary for consumer buying and housing activities
(Text Chapters 8-10)

Sheet	Actions to be taken	Planned completion date	Completed (√)

Sheet 70 — Summary for insurance activities

(Text Chapters 11-14)

Sheet	Actions to be taken	Planned completion date	Completed (√)

89

Sheet 71 — Summary for investment activities

(Text Chapters 15-19)

Sheet	Actions to be taken	Planned completion date	Completed (√)

Sheet 72 — Summary for retirement and estate planning activities
(Text Chapters 20-21)

Sheet	Actions to be taken	Planned completion date	Completed (√)